Opening up Respect

CW00376630

Opening up Respect brings together tried and tested practical classroom ideas and inspiring teaching and learning suggestions to support the important part that RE plays in the wider school aim of educating children to take their place in our diverse society. Over the past two years, the RE Today Advisers have found schools increasingly involved in teaching and learning about the child's place in school, local, national and global communities, and RE has been tremendously supportive in achieving this aim.

Most importantly children have had the opportunity to learn about and from people with ideas and beliefs different from their own.

Whilst RE cannot create a harmonious society, it can support children in modelling the skills of disagreeing respectfully, understanding difference and gaining core knowledge about why people from particular religions choose to hold different beliefs and ideas. This publication also highlights where religions share ideas and beliefs and can work together to support others.

Within this publication our youngest children are offered the opportunity to learn through the distancing device of a Querk, and using characters that could be sitting next to them in class to explore the assumptions we make about people from what we see on the outside. One of our popular visual resources shares the story of Yawtown and how the different religious communities respond to religious teaching to support a crisis. Older children can enquire into global communities by imagining the world community as 100 jelly babies! Finally, to support the subject leader and to facilitate an RE day in your school there is a step-by-step guide to running your own multifaith conference in school.

Fiona Moss

Imran

Grace

Arjan

Web links: RE Today website

The RE Today website offers subscribers some free additional resources and classroom-ready materials related to this publication. Look out for the 'RE Today on the web' logo at the end of selected articles.

To access resources:

- go to the RE Today website www.retoday.org.uk

- click on the **download login** button and use the password from this term's issue of *REtoday* magazine

- click on **Primary curriculum publication – web supplement**

- click on the title of the publication and scroll down the page to find what you are looking for.

IS IT IMPORTANT TO TREAT EVERYONE RESPECTFULLY?

For the teacher

The activities in this section enable children in the 4–6 age range to learn about the importance of being welcoming by sharing a Buddhist story of welcoming, listening to a Muslim story about disrespectful behaviour and exploring the importance of respect. These activities help children to understand the value placed on **community** and **respect for all** by people with religious beliefs.

Jo Crabtree, a religious education advanced skills teacher in Lancashire, has been developing the use of these resources with children from 4 to 6.

These activities are aimed at developing knowledge, skills and understanding in relation to:

- what it means to belong to a group
- the meaning of some stories told about religious leaders
- the importance of treating all people, including those who may be different from ourselves, with respect.

Although these activities are modelled using a Querk, all the activities can be employed in any classroom using more readily available teddy bear-like toys or perhaps a persona doll.

What is a Querk?

A Querk is a teddy-bear-like soft toy which is shaped to be cuddled! Querks look different from other soft toy which makes them unusual and special. They are initially inside 'eggs' from which, after a time, they 'hatch'. Querks are available commercially from Spectrum Educational.

See: www.spectrumeducational.co.uk

However, if you don't have a Querk, you can still engage in all the activities in this article. Choose a soft toy that is not likely to be owned by the children in your class. The egg can be recreated by using a child's pyjama case or hot water bottle cover.

What can children do as a result of this unit?

These pupil-friendly 'I can . . .' statements describe what pupils working at levels 1 and 2 may achieve through this work.

Level	Description of achievement: I can. . .
1	• **talk about** how the Buddha or the Prophet Muhammad showed respect
	• **respond to questions** arising from a story about respectful behaviour
	• *talk about* why welcoming people and showing them respect is a good idea.
2	• **identify the meaning** in the stories told about the Buddha and the Prophet Muhammad.
	• *respond, with thoughts of my own, to the stories and situations and suggest why respectful behaviour is important.*

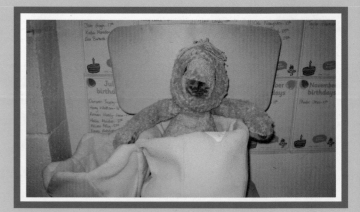

Links to Early Leaning goals

This work links to many of the Early Learning goals. There are specific links with Personal, Emotional and Social Development, communication, language and literacy and knowledge and understanding of the world. Subscribers can download a full list of the relevant Early Learning goals from the RE Today website.

Note: Muhammad is highly respected by Muslims and it is usual to say the blessing 'peace be upon him' after his name. In text such as this it is often abbreviated to 'pbuh' or the Arabic symbol ﷺ is used. This sign of respect should be inferred throughout this resource.

Activity 1   Welcoming a visitor

Arrange for the Querk inside its egg or an alternative toy hidden inside the 'egg' to be delivered in a large box to your classroom. Ensure the box has air holes. On the outside of the box there should be a note from Mummy Querk saying;

> Please look after this and open it in one week's time. Only open this parcel if you can look after the contents.

- Place the parcel on a shelf in the classroom.
- After a week has passed prepare to open the box.
- Encourage the children to speculate about what is inside. What might they need to do to look after the contents?
- Carefully remove the Querk egg from the box and take the Querk out of its egg.
- **Discuss** with the children how they can welcome the Querk and make him part of their class.
- Allow the Querk to become part of the daily life of the class. He may go to assembly, take part in circle time and provide someone for children to share their worries with.

Now move on to Activity 2.

Subscribers can download a short film clip from the RE Today website of Mummy Querk asking the children to look after her baby.

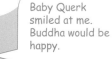

Baby Querk smiled at me. Buddha would be happy.

I left Sam out, Buddha would want me to play with her.

Activity 2   Feeling unwelcome

Following on from Activity 1, the class use the Querk to discuss ideas of their own, and ideas from a Buddhist story, about compassion, kindness and including all the members of a community.

- **Share with the children** an email that has been sent by Mummy Querk, see below. This email is also available as a film clip on the RE Today website.
- **Ask** the children to think about how the other Querks might be feeling.
- **Share the story** of Sunita and the scavenger with the children. A version of this story can be found on page 5. While they listen to the story ask the children to sit with their talk partners.
- **Ask the children to:**
  - **Think about** how Sunita felt at key points in the story
  - **Show** the emotions that Sunita felt on their faces and then draw them on the face outlines on page 4.

Now move on to Activity 3.

To: Pupils@yawtown.primary.sch.uk

Subject: Baby Querk

Hello Children,

I've heard that you are doing a very good job of looking after my little children. They are really happy and feel like part of your class family.

Did you know that two other classes have said they'd look after two more of my precious babies? They have settled in well but there is a bit of a problem that I need your help with. One of them is feeling lonely and a bit left out. When all the children go to assembly or to PE my young Querk is left behind and the children don't seem to like it. Where I live, no one gets left out, so we don't know what to do about it.

Please could you find out what different people think about leaving someone out, and help my baby to feel happier?

Thank you so much for your help.

Mummy Querk

Activity 3   Conscience Alley

Once Activity 2 has been completed, introduce the Conscience Alley activity to the class.

- **Choose a capable thinker** and speaker from the class to play the part of Sunita.

- **Set up an alleyway** of children in the classroom, and stand your volunteer playing Sunita at one end. The group of children standing on one side of the alley are going to give reasons why Sunita should be ignored by the people who live in the town and ignored by the Buddha. The group of children standing on the other side of the alley are going to suggest reasons why Sunita should be treated and spoken to well by everybody.

- **Ask** the volunteer to walk down the alley. S/he will receive comments in turn from children on either side. At the end, s/he waits and thinks while the children who formed the alleyway all sit down again. Now ask the volunteer how they think Sunita must have felt, being treated so badly.

- **Ask** the children to compare with their talk partner how Sunita felt, how Baby Querk in the class was feeling and how the other Querks who were not being welcomed might feel.

- **Work** together as a class to create an action plan of how to make baby Querk feel welcome.

- **Act** out these ideas in a small group with children taking it in turns to be Baby Querk and members of the class.

Conscience Alley

Conscience Alley

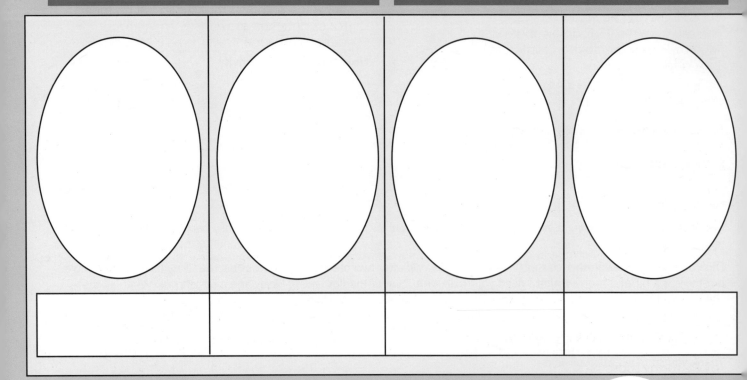

RE Today
Services

Sunita the Scavenger

Many years ago, when the Buddha was alive, there was a very poor man named Sunita living in a town in India. Sunita had a job as a road sweeper but he earnt so little money that he had no home. He slept by the side of the roads that he swept. He survived by being a scavenger, living on the food and belongings that other people threw out.

He was considered by the other people who lived in the town as the lowest of the low. They treated him as an outcast. Sunita watched other people enjoying their lives, buying food, laughing with their friends and going home to their families, but he wasn't allowed to join in. When a person who was from a higher caste, with a better job and more money passed him he had to scurry out of the way so that even his shadow didn't cross their path. Sometimes, when he was feeling tired or didn't notice someone walking towards him, he didn't move quickly enough and he was scolded by those around him. It was a hard and sad life. Sunita was miserable.

One day, when he looked up from his sweeping, he saw a large group of people approaching. It was the Buddha, a wise teacher, followed by thousands of people walking at the side of him and behind him. Sunita felt confused. He was full of joy at seeing the Buddha, but fearful too, as there was no way that he could move out of the road quickly enough. He stood quietly with his palms joined together in respect as the Buddha's procession came closer.

The Buddha smiled at Sunita and asked, 'My dear friend, would you like to leave your life and work here in the town and follow me?' Sunita immediately accepted the Buddha's offer. The Buddha made Sunita one of his monks, and for the rest of his life Sunita was treated with respect by whomever he met.

Source unknown

This story and the outline faces on page 4 are available for download by RE Today subscribers.
www.retoday.org.uk

RE Today
Services

Activity 4 Disrespectful behaviour

Use the Muslim story of the Thirsty Camel, and the Querk or other toy, to explore an example of disrespectful behaviour.

- **Explain** to the children, or they may notice for themselves, that the class Querk has gone missing.

- Arrange for a message to be sent from the headteacher requesting that all the other school Querks or persona dolls are sent to his or her office. **Speculate** with the children with the children about what might have happened. Is your class Querk with the head too?

- **Share** the Muslim story of the Thirsty Camel.

- **Ask** the children:

    - What disrespectful behaviour was shown in the story?

    - What was Muhammad trying to teach?

    - What could Muslims learn from this story?

- Arrange for another message from the head asking a child to come to the office to collect your class Querk. The headteacher will explain to the child that the Querk has been called names by the other Querks or persona dolls.

Now move on to Activity 5.

Muhammad and the Thirsty Camel

Prophet Muhammad was walking in a garden in Medina when he heard a strange noise. It sounded as if someone was crying. Muhammad found that the noise came from a very sad camel. The camel was crying because it was tied to a post in the hot sun without anything to drink.

Eventually, by stroking him and standing quietly behind him, Muhammad calmed the camel down. The camel realised that Muhammad would treat him well. The prophet became very angry – how dare someone treat the poor camel so badly? He searched for the owner, shouting loudly, 'Who owns this camel?'

Out of the shade of the biggest tree in the garden stepped a man, who was not thirsty or hot. Prophet Muhammad spoke quietly to the man reminding him that the camel was one of Allah's creatures. The camel worked hard for the man but he was not looking after the camel. The camel owner was ashamed. He had only been thinking about his own comfort, while his camel had been suffering. He had even upset the Prophet Muhammad.

From then on the camel owner treated all of Allah's creatures with the care and respect they deserved.

RE Today
Services

Activity 5 Respectful behaviour

When the Querk is brought back to the classroom the message is relayed that he has been treated disrespectfully by the other Querks.

- **Ask** the Querk how he has been treated but explain that he is too upset to respond.

- As a class, come up with examples of what disrespectful behaviour might be.

- Ask children, in small groups, to **freeze frame** examples of disrespectful behaviour. Ask those being treated disrespectfully how they feel.

- In talk, partners come up with three things that your Querk might expect for respectful behaviour. Record their ideas pictorially or with a key word on a mini whiteboard.

- Pair two sets of talk partners to share their ideas.

- Create a class list of disrespectful behaviour.

Continuous provision

During the week that these activities were going on with the whole class, one of the continuous provision activities was related to this work.

A selection of small world figures and dolls were made available and the children were asked to use them to act out situations where the figures were showing respectful behaviour.

Further questions that could be addressed using the Querks

Why is it important to listen to other people?

Is everyone important?

Where do we belong?

Why do I have to give things to other people?

Do our clothes make us different?

Activity 6 Sharing respect

Explain to the children that we need to share with the Querks who were being disrespectful some simple ways of showing respect.

Ask for ideas from the children as to how the message could be shared with the Querks. Your class will have their own ideas but one idea is outlined below.

- As a class, **design a poster** to be displayed in the other classroom showing examples of respectful behaviour. Ensure the poster shows at least one example that shows that they have learnt from the story in Activity 2 or 4.

- Ask your children to respond orally or by writing to the following **sentence starters:**

  Buddhists think behaving respectfully is important because . . .

  Muslims think behaving respectfully is important because . . .

  I think behaving respectfully is important because . . .

- Invite the other Querks and the headteacher into your classroom and tell them the story of your Querk. Give them the poster to display.

- In **Circle Time** pass your Querk around. As each child holds the Querk ask them to suggest one respectful thing they can do for someone they care for.

Continuous provision: acting out respectful behaviour with small world figures

WE'RE ALL DIFFERENT - WE'RE ALL THE SAME

Religious diversity for 5–7s

For the teacher

This set of learning ideas provide simple but thoughtful activities through which 5–7s can become increasingly at ease with religious difference.

There is a careful focus on enabling them to get beyond surface impressions. Looking at a friend for their 'inside' not just their 'outside' is an idea worth exploring in early primary learning in RE. These activities make it straightforward for the teacher to do this.

Activity Ia   Guess who?

Give each pair of children a set of ten labels and a copy of the five children on p.10.

Ask children to

- **talk** with a partner about which two labels they guess goes with each child.

- **explain** why they have made their choices, **justify** their guesses.

This activity is a good example of the literacy topic on labels, lists and captions in practice. It asks pupils to use reasoning skills in a 'speaking and listening' context.

Activity Ib   Meet the five children

Give children a copy of page 11.

- Ask a good reader to read out the speech bubbles that come from each of the five children.

- Ask all the pairs of children to move their labels round so that they match what the children say.

Talk about some ways in which we sometimes guess the wrong things about people from how they look.

For the 20 cards you might use or adapt these:

Brown eyes	Clever	Blonde hair	Smiley	Brave
Black skin	Thin	Red sweatshirt	Good at listening	Kind
Lots of freckles	Thoughtful	Friendly	Tall	Happy
Funny	Black shoes	Caring	Grey skirt	Curly hair

Achievements and outcomes

These pupil friendly 'I can . . .' statements suggest the learning outcomes that this work can yield.

Level   Description of achievement: I can. . .

1
- **name** some different religions
- **notice some simple features** of religion (e.g. going to a mosque)
- *talk about how we are all different and the feelings that go with the stories.*

2
- **retell a story** about what matters inside a person (story of Samuel and David)
- **identify some simple** features of religious belonging
- *respond sensitively to stories, characters and emotions*

Activity 2a   Inside and outside: what we can and can't see

Ask children to play a sorting game. Give children in pairs 20 cards that list and/or picture features of how we look, and of personality or 'inside' features.

Ask the pairs to discuss:

- which of these 20 things we can tell by looking at a person, and which we can only find out if we know the person.

- when they are grown up, which four of these would they like to be true about them?

- which matter most, the 'outside' or the 'inside'.

Children may be familiar with the saying 'Don't judge a book by its cover'. Talk with the class about what this means.

Activity 2b   A story about 'inside and outside'

The Jewish story of how David was chosen to be king of Israel when he was just a boy is over 3000 years old.

Read the story to the class from I Samuel 16 in the Bible.

The Prophet Samuel goes to the house of Jesse to select one of his sons to be King of Israel. He looks at Jesse's seven oldest boys: each one looks great, but God tells Samuel 'not that one'. David, looking rough and probably smelly from looking after the sheep, comes in. God says: 'Human beings look at the outward appearance, but God looks at the heart.' It is what is inside that matters most.

Talk to the children about the fact that we are all different, and we look different. Talk about the importance of what is 'inside' rather than what is 'outside'. What did young David need to be like on the inside if he was to be a good king? (Fair? Brave? Helpful to other people? Kind?).

RE Today
Services

Activity 3   Who does what?

The earlier activities familiarise the children with our five examples of children. This activity uses some thinking skills of ranking and connection to make some judgements and justify some choices. This is good work done completely as speaking and listening.

- Tell your class that all five of the children in the pictures are in the same class: Class 1A at Yawtown Primary School.

- Four special things are happening at school this year, and some children need to help. They need to decide which of the five children should be first choice to do each of the four special activities.

We have, of course, deliberately seeded some puzzles into the work.

- Tell the class about the four scenarios one by one, and ask them to talk with partners about which child should be chosen for the special role, and why.

Nativity play: taking the lead role

The school's Christmas play has several big parts, Perhaps the biggest is Mary, or perhaps not! What about Joseph, or the angel? When the teacher asks the children who would like to have a big part in the play, all five put their hands up straight away. She asks them to say why they would like a big part, and why they would be good at it. What do you think each child would say?

Possible answers

Arjan: 'I could be Joseph because I am in a drama group'.

Grace: 'I'd love to be Mary. I've never been Mary before.'

Hannah: 'Actually, Mary was a Jewish girl, and so am I. Or I could be an angel. I'm a good singer.'

Giving out the sweets at the Id assembly

When the Muslim festival of Id is celebrated, the Muslim families at the school send in sweets for everyone for a special assembly. The teacher is going to choose a child to give out the sweets to the class.

Possible answers

Imran: 'I really want to do this, because Id is my family's festival and my mum made the sweets.'

Arjan: 'I like sweets, and I like to be fair. I could do this!'

Hannah: 'Me and Grace could do this together.'

Making the learning clear

- When pupils have talked about who will be allowed to do what, then remind them that what is on the inside can be much more important than outside. Refer back to the biblical quote. We are all different, and one of these differences is religion. But we can all try hard, be thoughtful, show kindness.

- Give each child a heart shape, and ask them to choose words or draw simple pictures that show what they want to be like 'on the inside'. Can they speculate what Samit, Grace, Hannah, Arjan and Imran would put in their hearts?

An extra in a film

A new film is being made in Yawtown and the director has asked school if two children could appear as extras in the film. They won't have to speak, but they will be in several scenes in the background in a field of animals, and be seen in thousands of cinemas! He asks for children who are confident and helpful.

Possible answers

Arjan: 'I could do this very well. I'd like to be an actor.'

Grace: 'I'd like to be in a movie. I am a confident girl!'

Imran: 'Please can I be in the film? I'm really good at following instructions.'

Samit: 'I'm a helpful boy – just ask my Gran. And I'm good with animals.'

Flowers for the Queen

Her Majesty is visiting Yawtown for the day. A child is going to give her a bunch of flowers when she arrives, and someone from Class 1A is to be the child. It's not a difficult job, but a nice smile and a welcome are needed. The child who does this might be nervous, so it needs to be someone with a cool head!

Possible answers

Samit: 'I like older people like the Queen. I'd love to do it. It doesn't have to be a girl, you know.'

Hannah: 'I think it would be special to meet her Majesty. I will try hard to be careful and do it right.'

The following resources are available for download by RE Today subscribers.

- A visual presentation to support Activity 1b

- A set of cards to use for Activity 2a

- A set of teacher information on the five religions represented in this activity.

We are all different: You can't tell everything about a person by looking at them

Guess who . . .

is in Beavers	likes feeding the rabbits
says a prayer before eating dinner	likes football
plays the drums	likes making cards
is allowed to light a candle on a special day	reads lots of books
goes to drama club	lives with Gran, Mum and Dad

Imran   Grace   Samit   Hannah   Arjan

RE Today
Services

If the world was a community of 100 people. . .

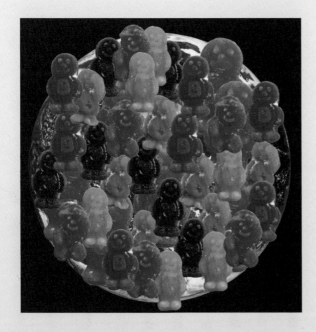

1

There are nearly 7 billion people on our planet. That's very hard to imagine, so just think what it would be like if the world was just one community of 100 people.

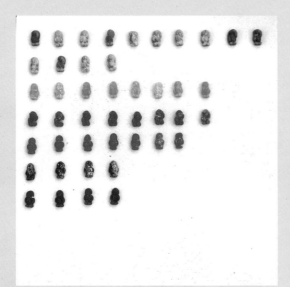

2

	60 of them would be Asian		8 would be Latin American
	14 would be African		5 would be from USA and Canada
	12 would be European		1 would be from Australia/NZ

3

	14 would speak Mandarin		7 would speak Spanish
	8 would speak Hindi or Urdu		4 would speak Russian
	8 would speak English		4 would speak Arabic
The remaining 55 would speak over 200 languages!			

4

	33 would be Christian		6 would be Buddhist
	22 would be Muslim		10 would belong to other religions
	15 would be Hindu		14 would not follow any religion

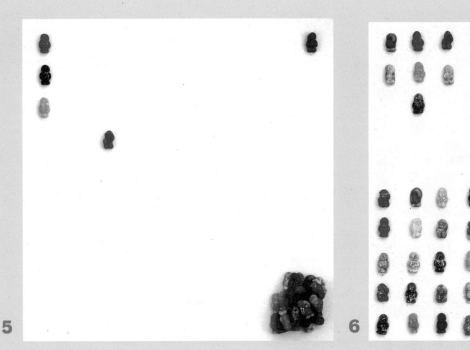

5

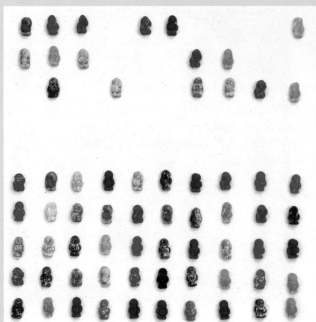

6

5 people would have 33% of all the wealth between them.

33 people would have 3% of the wealth between them.

17 people would not have safe, clean water to drink.

50 people would not have enough to eat every day.

The people without water are almost certainly among the hungry ones.

7

8

Only one would go to university.

7 people would own cars.

7 people would own computers.

They would probably be the same people.

RE Today
Services

Activity 1 Ask questions

Use the images to encourage pupils to talk. You might select two, bearing in mind that 1–4 are to do with diversity and 5–8 to do with fairness and justice.

a They should **reflect** on the information and raise as many questions as they can think in response.

b Ask pupils to sort through and analyse the questions: which ones are good questions? Which ones only have one right answer or many possible answers?

   • Which ones are about understanding the images? (e.g. Do the colours match across the pictures?)

   • Which ones would need some specialist knowledge? (e.g. What different types of Christians are there?)

   • Which ones use your imagination? (e.g. How might the 33 people in picture 5 feel about the five with the wealth?)

   • Which ones open up a good enquiry? (e.g. How should we live in a community with lots of differences?)

c **Evaluate** the questions: which one is the best question to explore?

Now move on to Activities 2–6.

The following activities explore the question: 'In a community with many differences, how should we live?' They may be adapted to address other questions that your pupils raise.

Activity 2 Investigate the issues

Talk about what it would be like to live in a community of 100 like this.

Ask pupils to work in groups. Ask them to think of **four benefits** of living in this community, and **four difficulties** that might arise.

Discuss these as a class. Do the benefits outweigh the difficulties?

Activity 3 Interpret religious sources

The texts of page 24 give some of the commands that different religions have to help people live in harmony. Copy these on to card, cut them up and give groups of pupils a set each.

Ask pupils to take 3 or 4 of these texts and

• suggest what they mean

• think of two things that would go well in the community of 100 if people followed these ideas.

Report back and discuss.

Activity 4 Similarities and differences

Give pupils a blank T-shirt outline (example available to subscribers on RE Today website). Ask groups of pupils to design two T-shirts. Using the information on page 24, pupils need to think about what these different groups have in common and what belief they hold that is distinctive.

• One T-shirt should have a rule on it that all the people in the community might agree with.

• One T-shirt should have a rule that might only apply to one identified belief group in the community.

You may wish to give pupils additional information on some religious and non-religious beliefs for this. The purpose of the unit is to see the need for co-operation and peaceful co-existence, but this activity reminds pupils of the differences that remain.

Activity 5 Evaluating the impact

a Gather the T-shirt commands pupils have come up with.

   As a class, choose the five most important rules for the community of 100. For each one, make links with at least one religious text.

   • One rule must be to do with handling disagreement – how well people get on when, for example, one person believes in God and one person doesn't.

   • One rule must be to do with justice and fairness.

   As a class, discuss whether you can agree on five rules. What would you do with people who did not keep the rules?

b Imagine that the World 100 Community is producing a leaflet to advertise itself, just in case other life forms might come and visit this remarkable community. Ask pupils to write a blurb of 100–150 words, describing the way of life based on the five key rules. Explain what kind of behaviour and attitudes would be shown in the community.

Activity 6 Express and apply

Share the sample writing frame and sentence starters on page 25 to help pupils to express their own responses to this unit in a structured piece of writing.

How shall we live in community? What do people say?

A man once asked the Prophet Muhammad what was the best thing in Islam, and he replied, 'It is to feed the hungry and to give the greeting of peace both to those you know and to those you do not know.'

Islam: Hadith of Bukhari

All people are responsible for one another.

Judaism: Talmud, Sanhedrin 27b

Love the Lord your God with all your heart, all your soul and all your strength.
Love your neighbour as you love yourself.

Judaism and Christianity: Deuteronomy 6:5 and Leviticus 19:18

When you do things, do not let selfishness or pride be your guide. Instead, be humble and give more honour to others than to yourselves. Do not be interested only in your own life, but be interested in the lives of others.

Christianity: Philippians 2:3-4 (NCV)

And what does the LORD require of you? To act justly and to love mercy and to walk humbly with your God.

Judaism and Christianity: Micah 6:8

Giving simply because it is right to give, without thought of return, is enlightened giving. Giving with regrets, or in the expectation of receiving some favour or of getting something in return, is selfish giving.

Hinduism: Bhagavad Gita 17.20-21

Whenever you see someone else hungry or thirsty or a stranger or naked or sick or in prison and do not look after them, you do not look after me, said Jesus.

Christianity: Matthew 25:31-46

Happy is the person who finds fault with himself instead of finding fault with others.

Islam: Hadith

Love your enemies and pray for those who persecute you.

Christianity: Matthew 5:43

Conquer anger by love.
Conquer wickedness by goodness.
Conquer the stingy by giving.
Conquer the liar by truth.

Buddhism: Dhammapada 223

Let your aims be common
and your hearts united,
and all of you be of one mind,
so you may live well together.

Hinduism: Rig Veda 10.191.4

Treat others as you would wish to be treated.

The Golden Rule: all religions have a version of this, as do many people who do not follow a religion or believe in God.

The only possible basis for a sound morality is mutual tolerance and respect: tolerance of one another's customs and opinions; respect for one another's rights and feelings; awareness of one another's needs.

Non-religious: A J Ayer, The Humanist Outlook

There is no greater penance than patience, no greater happiness than contentment, no greater evil than greed, no greater virtue than mercy, and no more potent weapon than forgiveness.

Sikhism: Guru Amardas

Applying the learning: living in community

Use the following five-paragraph structure to write a short response to what you have learned about living in a world of difference. Choose at least two sentence starters from each box.

1 My reaction

When I learned about the world as a community of 100 people . . .

I was surprised that . . .

I realised that . . .

The images made me think that . . .

The most interesting image was . . . because . . .

2 Understanding the information

If the world was a community of 100 people the best things would be . . .

The most challenging things would be . . .

This is like the world because . . .

This is like/not like my own community because . . .

3 Evaluating religious ideas

Religions are concerned with how people live together because . . .

The best teachings help because . . . for example . . .

If people kept the teaching from . . . [religion] to . . . , then . . .

The best teaching for helping people to handle differences is . . . because . . .

If people disagree, they could follow the teaching . . . so that . . .

4 Weighing up my thoughts

Some people might agree with the teaching . . . because . . .

Some people might disagree with the teaching . . . because . . .

For me the most important thing about living in a world of difference is . . .

My thinking has been helped by learning about the world as a community of 100 because . . .

The religious teachings have helped my thinking because . . .

5 Applying these ideas to the world and to myself

The world would be a better place if . . .

My town would be a better place if . . .

Religious believers could help make the world a better place if . . .

People without religious beliefs could help make the world a better place if . . .

If I was to do one thing differently in my life now it would be . . . because . . .

RE Today
Services

PLANNING A MULTIFAITH CONFERENCE IN YOUR SCHOOL

For the teacher

Planning a multifaith conference, whether for your school, or involving other local schools, might seem daunting! This article is designed to provide a lot of practical guidance, tips, creative ideas – and reassurance! With careful planning, well-chosen workshop leaders, and appropriate activities, this is the type of event which will stay with pupils for many years, both what they did and what they learned.

The examples, comments and photographs included in these pages come from a variety of multifaith conferences, workshop leaders and teachers who are committed to providing pupils with opportunities to experience such events. We hope they can inspire you to plan one for your school!

See also

1 What is RE?
A six-minute film from NATRE about Primary RE, including clips from a multifaith event for primary schools.
See: www.natre.org.uk/explore/video.php?id=47

2 Herefordshire Primary Schools Multi Faith Project
Pupils who took part in a multifaith day present their thoughts on what happened and their feelings about the day.
See: www.hereford-edu.org.uk/faith/default.asp?PG_ID=1&GRP_ID=1

3 Religious Believers Visiting Schools
A free downloadable leaflet from NATRE provides guidance and a code of conduct for visitors to schools.
See: www.natre.org.uk/free.php

4 BBC Learning Zone Broadband Clips Library
A vast searchable database of short clips on many aspects of religion and belief designed for use in the classroom.
See: www.bbc.co.uk/learningzone/clips

5 CLEO
A large collection of high-quality videos specially filmed to support RE and featuring a variety of religions and beliefs.
See: www.cleo.net.uk

6 *Exploring Religion Around Me:* a collection of tried and tested curriculum activities, including interviews with eight young people from different religious traditions (ed. Joyce Mackley, RE Today Services, ISBN 978-1-904024-96-5)
See: www.retoday.org.uk

7 *Exploring Codes for Living:* a collection of tried and tested curriculum activities, including the Commitment Game and activities exploring the Golden Rule (ed. Joyce Mackley, RE Today Services, ISBN 978-1-905893-07-2)
See: www.retoday.org.uk

Razwan-Ul-Haq, teacher, artist and writer, leads a workshop on Muslim art (above) and **Sandra Millar,** Children's Officer, Diocese of Gloucester, leads a workshop on biblical storytelling(below).

What can children do as a result of this unit?

The following pupil friendly 'I can . . .' statements describe the learning that may be expected of pupils in the 9–11 age range

Level	Description of achievement: I can. . .
3	• **describe** what someone from a religion I have found out about might do to show their commitment to their religion
	• *make links between some of the commitments religious people have and some things I am committed to.*
4	• **use the right words to describe** examples of what is important to followers of two of the religions I have studied
	• *respond meaningfully to the idea of commitment, showing that I understand the impact of religion on everyday life.*
5	• **explain** some ways that the teaching of a religion connects with the individual's choices about their way of life
	• *express my own views about the challenges that commitment to a religious way of life brings to ordinary people.*

RE Today
Services

Planning the event

1 When should I start planning?

Early planning is a key priority for a successful and relatively stress-free event. A six-month lead time is recommended – this gives appropriate time to get the workshop leaders you want booked, plan the programme and the practical details, and build the event into the whole school curriculum so that pupils experience the event in a suitable context to enhance and progress learning in RE.

Ideally you will need a team of people to organise the event. If your event involves other schools then you have an even wider group of people whose expertise you can draw on. Members of your SACRE may also be able to help.

2 What do I want pupils to get out of the day?

It is important to be clear from the outset what learning outcomes you are looking for. How does the event link to the locally agreed syllabus for RE, or other statutory syllabus being followed, and enable pupils to demonstrate progression in learning in RE? How does the event link to the wider curriculum?

A multifaith conference is to do with a memorable, positive and creative encounter with people from a variety of faith communities, not about collecting facts.
Expressing learning outcomes in pupil-friendly 'I can . . .' statements helps keep the focus on the RE learning. Answering these questions will help you identify the theme for the conference.

3 What about a venue?

Ideally you will need a school with a supportive headteacher, a hall and 3–4 workshop rooms which are available for the whole day. If your own school is unable to host the event, consider working with another local school which is able to provide facilities.

4 How do I choose workshop leaders?

Good workshop leaders are not just representatives of the religions chosen for the event: they must also be skilled at working with young people in ways that are engaging, creative and in line with the highest expectations of the school.

Good workshop leaders: understand that the workshop is not about imparting facts or the history of their religion, but about a personal encounter; know how to plan a workshop which has a clear focus, maintains appropriate pace, and is appropriate for the given age and ability range; expect the schools to brief them in detail about what is expected of them.

Colleagues in other schools, your local SACRE, RE Today or a professional association such as NATRE will often be able to recommend individuals whom you can approach with confidence.

Butta Singh, a Sikh teacher, leading a workshop on Sikh music.

What do workshop leaders want to know?

Six experienced workshop leaders told us what they would like to happen in advance of the event:

- pupils to have given some thought to attitudes to other religions

- conference to focus on three or more religions

- time built in at the end of each workshop for pupils to reflect and record their thoughts

- pupils encouraged to ask questions, no matter how trivial

- other members of staff briefed so they know who the new people in school that day are and what they are doing

- workshop leaders told the size, age and ability of the pupils, and any curriculum focus they want the workshop leaders to build on or lead in to so they can prepare appropriately

- workshop leaders asked what equipment they need for their presentation (e.g. whiteboard, internet access, computer), and advised on space and layout of the room

- the event to be thought of as a springboard to other things, not stand-alone.

Six workshop leaders from five religious traditions (Bahá'í, Hindu, Jain, Muslim and Sikh) enjoying lunch together.

Planning the event

5 What about funding?

Good workshop leaders will need to be paid and there are various costs related to equipment, materials, administration and refreshments. Consider:

- contributions from each participating school
- fundraising by the PTA
- if sessions involve activities such as dance, music or art (which they should do as the workshops need to be creative), then this might release funding
- other schools might be able to contribute some funding if they can have access to some of the footage filmed on the day, or can take part in the day by video conference.

6 What preparation is needed for the teachers and other adults taking part?

It's important to remember that not all colleagues may be comfortable with the idea of the conference and will need to be enabled to take an effective part. It is important that they are participants on the day, not observers.

Consider this an opportunity for staff development, perhaps by leading a session in a staff meeting for all staff with the conference and what it is aiming to achieve as a main focus.

7 What preparation do pupils need?

At the conference pupils will be meeting new pupils and adults, and may be doing so in the context of a strange school. A preparatory activity which generates discussion and questions for the day is crucial, for example about what matters to them and to others. Questions identified can be sent in advance to the workshop leaders so they can build them into their planning (see page 29).

8 What about permission forms?

If you are planning to film on the day with a view to using the outcomes in reporting on the event (e.g. school newsletter, school website, local press) then you will need to obtain the signed consent of parents for use of the images of their children, and also of the other adults taking part.

9 What follow-up activities could pupils do?

It is crucial that pupils undertake some form of follow-up work to demonstrate their understanding and help embed the learning. Some suggestions are given on page 33.

10 How can I evaluate the event?

Obtaining feedback from the pupils, staff and workshop leaders is important in helping to identify whether the intended learning outcomes of the day have been achieved – and to aid planning your next conference! Some pupil responses to one conference are given on page 33. It will be after the follow-up activities have been completed that a truer picture of what has been achieved will be evident.

Jane Silver-Corren, a Jewish educator, leading a workshop on Judaism, with adults and children taking part in a wedding dance.

What advice would workshop leaders give to someone from their own faith community taking part in a similar event?

Six experienced workshop leaders told us:

- Make it practical and interactive, and lots of fun.

- Talk about your own experience of your faith, not details that pupils can find in books.

- Let the school know that you are open to any questions, so that they can prepare pupils.

- Include pictures, photos and artefacts which pupils can see and touch, and ask questions about. Use short video clips too, if possible.

- Be proactive in asking the school for information about the event, the pupils (age, ability, number, etc) and the theme of the event.

- It is a good opportunity to strengthen one's own faith by philosophically and thoughtfully considering the points of view of others.

Midge Ault, primary teacher and Bahá'í representative on SACRE, leading a workshop on creating a dance to express the value of unity.

RE Today Services

Preparing pupils

Activities for pupils

Asking pupils to complete one or more activities in advance of the conference will help ensure that they are well-prepared both to contribute to the event's success and to deepen their learning. The two activities on these pages are illustrative of the sort that prepares pupils well, and provides insights and questions to forward to the workshop leaders so they can plan with this in mind.

1 Talking Circle

Arrange the classroom in an inner and outer circle of chairs so that all pupils can sit facing one other person. Give each pupil a sheet with the nine quotations below. They talk about one of the quotations with the pupil sitting opposite them for two minutes. They should: read the quote aloud together; each say what they think it means; say whether they agree with it; mark their sheet to show what they thought. The sheet of quotations is available for download from the RE Today website for subscribers.

The outer circle then moves round one place so that everyone faces a new partner, with whom they talk about another quotation. This is a clearly structured activity which builds confidence and provides support for learning.

2 The Values Game

This game is an activity best played by pupils in groups of four. It asks pupils to consider and justify the importance of 30 values. It gives pupils an opportunity to discuss a range of opinion, giving reasons for their own beliefs and respecting those of others. The board and cards for the game are printed on pages 30 and 31, and are also available for subscribers to download from the RE Today website. The rules for the game are printed with the cards.

You will need to make a board and set of cards for each group of four pupils; these are available on RE Today's website for subscribers, or pages 30 and 31 may be photocopied. The board should be blown up to A3 size.

A third activity, The Commitment Game, is found in *Exploring Codes for Living*, ed Joyce Mackley, RE Today Services, ISBN 978-1-905893-07-2, and is also available as a free download for subscribers.

Bharti Tailor, trainer, Hindu Chaplain and Secretary General of the Hindu Forum of Britain, sharing a blessing with pupils after she has demonstrated worship round the shrine.

The following resources are available for subscribers to download from the RE Today website.

- A copy of the board and cards for The Values Game
- A sheet of quotations for Talking Circle
- A template for the Human Bingo activity

See: www.retoday.org.uk

By following the teachings of Buddha, [people] do not give way to greed, anger or foolishness, but live peaceful lives of kindness and wisdom, without killing or stealing. The Teaching of the Buddha	God's Spirit makes us loving, happy, peaceful, patient, kind, good, faithful, gentle and self-controlled. There is no law against behaving in any of these ways. Bible, Galatians 5:22–23	These six one should never give up: truthfulness, generosity, good humour, friendliness, forgiveness and contentment. Mahabharata, 5:33
A man once asked the Prophet what was the best thing in Islam, and the latter replied: 'It is to feed the hungry and to give the greeting of peace both to those you know and to those you do not know.' Hadith of Bukhari (Islam)	Do not store up treasures on earth! Moths and rust can destroy them, and thieves can steal them. Instead store up your treasures in heaven, where moths and rust cannot destroy them, and thieves cannot steal them. Your heart will always be where your treasure is. Bible, Matthew 6:19	I, the Lord, command you to do what is just and right. Protect the person who is being cheated from the person who is cheating him. Do not ill-treat or oppress foreigners, orphans or widows; and do not kill innocent people. Hebrew Bible, Jeremiah 22:3
Treat other people as you would like them to treat you. The Golden Rule	No one of you is a believer until he desires for his brother that which he desires for himself. A saying of the Prophet, Number 13 of Imam Al-Nawawi's Forty Hadiths	No one shall cause another pain or injury: all shall live in peace together. Guru Granth Sahib

THE VALUES GAME

Ultimate value

World shatteringly valuable

Extremely valuable

Valuable

Fairly valuable

Not completely useless

cards

RE Today
Services

The Values Game

How to play this game:

1 You will need a board and a set of cards, and it works well if you play the game in a group of four.

2 Put the cards in pile, face downwards. Play in turns around the group.

   When it's your turn, you must do three things:

   - **Read out the top card**

   - **Ask the other players where on the board they would put the card, and why.**

   - **Ignore them, and put it where you think it goes for you. Give your reasons to the group.**

3 When it's your turn, if you want to, you can also move another person's card to a space that you choose. 'Move one, place one' is the rule. It's important to give your reasons, and to negotiate if the space you want is already taken with another card.

4 All cards must be in one space only – no overlapping is allowed.

5 When all the cards are out, play three more rounds in which you just swap two cards over. Give your reasons.

Success	Empathy	Goodness	Honesty	Creativity	Devotion to God
Beauty	Sticking with it	Wealth	Learning	Strength of mind	Wisdom
Gratitude	Peace	Justice	Love	Commitment	Forgiveness
Concern for others	Equality	Loyalty	Kindness	Gentleness	Freedom
Acceptance	Self-control	Tradition	Tolerance	Hope	Humility

HARD TEST Scot Symon watches as an Inter Milan official inspects the Ibrox pitch ahead of the European Cup quarter-final second leg in March 1965

MAD FOR IT Ken MacCormack, 12, heads to Spain in October 1963 for the European Cup clash with Real Madrid

TO NUREMBERG
AND BEYOND...

It was a case of so near, yet so far for Rangers in Europe as the 1960s
came to a close but the fans enjoyed the journey as glory grew ever nearer

WEDNESDAY
29 MARCH
7.30 p.m.

THE RANGERS

FOLLOW FOLLOW
The Bridgeton Rangers
Supporters Club pose for
snaps as they prepare to
head off to Germany for
the 1967 European Cup
Winners' Cup final
against Bayern Munich

17

ROGER AND OUT A Roger Hynd goal is disallowed in the 1-0 loss to Bayern Munich in the Cup Winners' Cup Final in Nuremberg in May 1967

KAI AND MIGHTY Kai Johansen beats Borussia Dortmund keeper Bernhard Wessel in a 2-1 win in 1966

DRAGONS' DEN Dennis Setterington nets in a 4-0 Ibrox romp over Glentoran in the Cup Winners Cup in 1966

OOR WILLIE Slavia Sofia keeper S Simeonov is beaten by Willie Hende as Gers secure a 2-0 aggregate vic the Cup Winners Cup semi-final in 1

18

THE period from 1966 to 1969 saw Rangers go agonisingly close to lifting silver on the stage they craved most of all – Europe.

In season 1966-67, with Scot Symon at the helm, the club embarked on a Cup Winners' Cup campaign bookmarked with stunning highs, but which finished on an all-time low.

They dispatched Glentoran, Borussia Dortmund, Real Zaragoza and Slavia Sofia to set up a date with German giants Bayern Munich.

Six days earlier, in Lisbon, Celtic had piled the pressure on by becoming the first British team to win the European Cup.

Victory for Rangers in Nuremberg would have seen both European trophies heading to the same city in the same season for the first time.

But the weight of expectation wasn't just confined to their rivals, Scottish football had never been in ruder health as the final rolled around on May 31, 1967.

Scotland had beaten World Champions England at Wembley the previous month, Dundee United had knocked Barcelona out of the Fairs Cup while Kilmarnock reached the semi-final of the same tournament before losing to Leeds United.

These were heady days for Scotland's footballing sons but, unfortunately, Rangers would take the sting in the tale.

A shock defeat in the Scottish Cup to Berwick Rangers in the January had seen chairman John Lawrence announce club legends Jim Forrest and George McLean would never play for the club again. Alex Willoughby had stepped into the team and done a fine job, scoring 17 goals in three months.

However, with everything on the line in Nuremberg, manager Symon dropped Willoughby and played defender Roger Hynd in only his fourth match for the Light Blues – as a striker.

The move backfired and Rangers, struggling to threaten the Germans with a powder-puff attack, went down 1-0 in extra-time – Franz Roth scoring the winner.

Symon would leave the manager's position the following November, the burden of Berwick and Bayern proving too heavy a weight to carry.

The following two campaigns brought fine play but, again, Rangers couldn't quite scale the peak.

English clubs became their nemesis in 1968 and 1969 as Leeds beat them in the Fairs Cup quarter-finals and Newcastle did the same a year later in the last four. Heaven would have to wait...

ON HYND LEGS Roger Hynd challenges Sofia keeper Simeonov in May 1967 as Gers march on to the Cup Winners' Cup final in Nuremburg

RON OUR WAY Ronnie McKinnon is hugged by fans after a 1-0 home win over Slavia Sofia in May 1967 earns a place in the Cup Winners Cup Final

MAKESHIFT PHYSIO A fan is treated on the pitch after chaos at the Gallowgate end as Rangers crash out of the Fairs Cup at Newcastle

NO WAY PAST Newcastle's Willie McFaul and John McNamee squeeze out Colin Stein as Rangers draw 0-0 in the Fairs Cup semi-final first leg at Ibrox in May 1969

TOON BLOW Ronnie McKinnon tackles Bryan Robson in the 2-0 loss at Newcastle in 1969

THIN BLUE LINE Police move in as crowd trouble mars the 2-0 defeat to Newcastle in the Fairs Cup semi-final second leg

MISSED CHANCE Andy Penman fails to cash in on a golden chance for Rangers against Newcastle at Ibrox in 1969 as his penalty is saved by McFaul

FAIRS PAIR Andy Penman and Alex Ferguson, right, arrive back in Glasgow after a 2-0 loss to Leeds in the Inter-Cities Fairs Cup in April 1968

STEIN SEALER Colin Stein rams a late goal past Atletico Bilbao keeper Angel Iribar to make it 4-1 to Rangers in the quarter-final of the Inter-Cities Fairs Cup in March 1969

21

997
y
ston

BLUES BROTHERS The
legends of 72 gather again
as Rangers take on their
old foes Moscow Dinamo
in the UEFA Cup in 2001

RANGERS RHAPSODY
The Ibrox crowd salute
their heroes as a pipe
band leads the victorious
team around the stadium
as they show off the
European Cup Winners'
Cup with captain John
Greig proudly raising the
trophy aloft, above

THE BUILDING BLOCKS OF GLORY

After Barcelona, Rangers hearts and minds would turn to
the European Cup but the holy grail remained elusive

**THERE'S SNOW
GAME TONIGHT**
March 1979 and
Rangers' European Cup
tie against Cologne at
half-built new-look
Ibrox is postponed
due to the weather

RANGERS EUROPEAN ADVENTURES

THE fabric of Rangers would change forever during the period from 1972 to 1990 with the arrival of Graeme Souness and the rebuilding of Ibrox into an all-seated fortress.

But the holy grail remained the same – the European Cup. With the Cup Winners' Cup safely ensconced in the Blue Room, the club's position as a giant of the game was now confirmed.

However, a year's ban from European competition on the back of the trouble following the 1972 final, brought about a hangover that lasted for years on the big stage.

On the pitch, the club's reputation proceeded them and smaller sides upped their game when the famous Glasgow Rangers came to town.

After a disappointing three seasons, Rangers attacked the 1978-79 European Cup campaign with renewed vigour. The Scottish Treble had been won a matter of months before and a first-round draw against Juventus did nothing to dampen the enthusiasm.

The Old Lady of Italian football had reached the last four the previous season but they would make a hasty exit in September 1978. After going down 1-0 in Italy, Rangers achieved a European first, progressing after losing the first-leg of a continental tie.

Ibrox was a heaving wall of noise and colour as goals from Alex MacDonald and Gordon Smith put Rangers into the second round and the thought persisted that this could be their year on the grandest of stages.

The second-round draw did little to dissuade Rangers fans of the notion as Holland's PSV came out the hat and were duly dispatched thanks to a famous 3-2 win in Eindhoven – the Dutch side's first-ever home defeat in Europe.

Sadly, injuries and poor form caught up with John Greig's team after the winter break and Cologne sent the Light Blues home to think again in the quarter-finals.

The following years were barren and while the club was resurrected domestically after the arrival of Souness, success on the European stage proved almost impossible.

Memorable ties against Inter Milan in 1984 and Bayern Munich in 1989 set pulses racing but ultimately, the chase for domestic glory was all-consuming as Rangers went from strength to strength in Scotland.

BEAT SCHU AT LAST Cologne No.1 Harald Schumacher can't keep Tommy McLean's shot out as Rangers striker Billy Urquhart rushes in to make sure in a 1-1 draw but Gers go out at the quarter final stage of the European Cup 2-1 on aggregate in March 1979

DUTCH DATE Cutty Young, Tommy McLean and Alex MacDonald return from Holland in January 1973. Gers lost 3-1 at Ibrox to Ajax in the first-ever Super Cup Final before going down 3-2 in the second leg in Amsterdam

NO LUCK FOR THE IRISH Colin Stein and Graham Fyfe celebrate a Joe Burke own goal during a 4-1 win over Bohemians in the first round of the European Cup in September 1975

BERNE BLAST Colin Jackson fires in an overhead kick against Young Boys of Berne in a 1-0 win in the Cup Winners' Cup qualifying round in August 1977

SWISS SWEAT Sandy Jardine wins the ball against FC Zurich in a 1-1 draw at Ibrox in the first round of the European Cup in September 1976

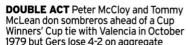

PRAISE THE GORD Colin Jackson watches as Gordon Smith's header at Ibrox earns a 2-1 aggregate win over Juventus in the European Cup first round in September 1978

DOUBLE ACT Peter McCloy and Tommy McLean don sombreros ahead of a Cup Winners' Cup tie with Valencia in October 1979 but Gers lose 4-2 on aggregate

BET ON RED Bobby Russell hails Ian Redford after his late Ibrox goal spares Rangers' blushes against Bohemians as they go through to the UEFA Cup second round 4-3 on aggregate in October 1984

GOAL MACHINE Ally McCoist scores in a shock 3-2 defeat at Bohemians in 1984, left, and the goalden boys who hit 18 goals against Valetta in Cup Winners' Cup in 1983, below. Clockwise from far left, Ian Redford, Ally Dawson, Dave Mitchell, Craig Paterson, Billy Mackay, John MacDonald, Davie McPherson and Robert Pritz

UP BOR IT Craig Paterson jumps with Borussia Dortmund's keeper as John MacDonald looks on in a 2-0 UEFA Cup win in September 1982

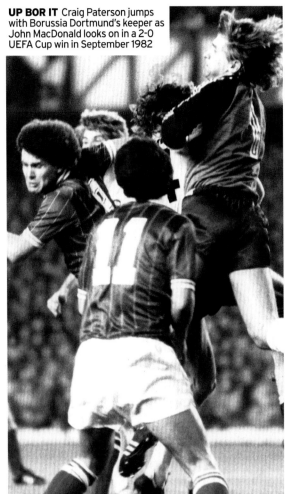

AYR REDY Ian Redford challenges the Cologne keeper in a 2-1 win in the UEFA Cup second round in October 1982

RANGERS EUROPEAN ADVENTURES

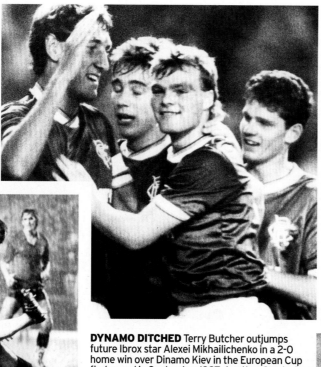

RED-HOT ROBERT Terry Butcher, Ally McCoist and Ian Durrant hail hat-trick hero Robert Fleck in a 4-0 UEFA Cup win over Finnish side Ilves in September 1986 and, below, McCoist is denied by Osasuna's Spanish keeper Jose Biurrun a year earlier in the same competition

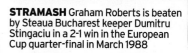

STRAMASH Graham Roberts is beaten by Steaua Bucharest keeper Dumitru Stingaciu in a 2-1 win in the European Cup quarter-final in March 1988

DYNAMO DITCHED Terry Butcher outjumps future Ibrox star Alexei Mikhailichenko in a 2-0 home win over Dinamo Kiev in the European Cup first round in September 1987. Another Ger-to-be Oleg Kuznetsov is busy pushing Jimmy Nicholl

MUD AND GUTS Osasuna keeper Jose Biurrun denies Cammy Fraser in a 1-0 UEFA Cup win in September 1985

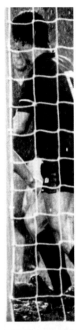

TOUGH AT TOP Player boss Graeme Souness slides in against Steaua Bucharest in 1988

SO HARD TO BEAR
Stuart McCall, Richard Gough, Ally McCoist and Ian Durrant show their torment after a 0-0 Ibrox draw with CSKA Moscow saw Rangers narrowly fail to make the final of the 1992 Champions League

CHASING THE DREAM

In season 1991-92, Rangers came within a whisker of a European Cup Final
as UEFA's new-look Champions League competiton set Ibrox pulses racing

THE 1992-93 European Cup arrived with a new name and a shiny logo as the tournament was rebranded as the UEFA Champions League. The group stages had appeared the season before as Barcelona won the big cup for the first time, beating Sampdoria 1-0 at Wembley in the final.

And in the heady days of the spring of 1993, it appeared that Rangers might finally live the dream.

Walter Smith's all-conquering vintage were simply unstoppable on home soil and they turned their attentions to the big boys' playground drawing Danish champs Lyngby in the first round. Two rounds had to be negotiated before sides could take their place in one of two four-team groups, the winners of which would contest the final.

Mark Hateley and Pieter Huistra were on target to give Rangers a 2-0 first-leg win at Ibrox which was followed by a 1-0 away win in Denmark, Ian Durrant grabbing the late goal to send the Ibrox men marching into a battle of Britain against Leeds United.

In a pulsating clash at Ibrox, Rangers recovered from the shock of a first-minute goal from United skipper Gary McAllister to win 2-1 and set up a famous return leg.

Ally McCoist and Hateley put the English champs to the sword in front of a hostile Elland Road – away fans were banned for both legs – and Eric Cantona's consolation was an irrelevance on a famous night for Rangers and Scottish football. The group stages had been reached and when the Light Blues came out the hat with Marseille, Brugge and CSKA Moscow, hopes were high that this could be the Ibrox club's year at last.

The first game did little to convince Ibrox fans otherwise as Marseille crumbled under the weight of a seething Govan crowd to surrender a two-goal lead, battered senseless by a stirring Rangers comeback in the last 14 minutes.

Goals from Gary McSwegan and Hateley earned a 2-2 draw and that was followed with a 1-0 win over CSKA in Bochum thanks to Ian Ferguson's solitary strike.

Momentum was with Gers now and back-to-back ties with Brugge brought four points as Scott Nisbett's deflected winner at home almost blew the roof off Ibrox.

A 1-1 draw in the return with the French champions set up tense finish to Group A. A victory over CSKA would send Rangers to their first-ever European Cup Final – if Marseille failed to beat Brugge.

But on a night of missed chances, Smith's side just couldn't get over the line and drew 0-0 while Marseille won 1-0 at Brugge.

The sickening blow was even harder to swallow when the French went on to dump Milan in the final before becoming embroiled in a match-fixing scandal. Marseille owner Bernard Tapie was found guilty of bribing Valenciennes to win a match and tie up the French title quicker in order to have more to prepare for the final against Milan. They were stripped of the French title.

HEAVEN AND ELL Ally McCoist makes it 2-0 at Elland Road in November 1992. Leeds made it 2-1 but Gers went through to the Champions League Group Stage

ON A LYNG AND A PRAYER Nigerian defender Emeka Ezeugo denies McCoist as Rangers beat Danish side Lyngby 2-0 in September 1992 in the first round of the Champions League

BEST OF BRITISH Mc away at Ibrox after mak against Leeds in last-16 League first-leg tie in O

MARKED MAN Mark Hateley battles with Jon Newsome at Elland Road after making it 1-0

LEEDING FROM THE START Lee Chapman, Eric Cantona and Gordon Strachan mob first-minute scorer Gary McAllister after the goal that silenced the Ibrox crowd in the opening leg but Gers fought back to win 2-1

49

AFTER the glory and the agony of 1993, the rich man's playground of the Champions League became the benchmark for a club desperate to shine in Europe. And shine they did.

Rangers would never again come so close to lifting the trophy but they became regulars at the top table and a trip to the lion's den of Govan was a tie to be feared by the biggest in the game.

The famous scalps roll off the tongue – Parma were battered 2-0 at Ibrox in the 1999 UCL final qualifying round with Dutchman Dick Advocaat now in charge and that campaign also gave a double bloody nose to PSV Eindhoven who were defeated 1-0 in Holland and destroyed 4-1 in Glasgow.

Bayern Munich survived a trip to Scotland but a screamer from Jorg Albertz in a 1-1 draw blew the roof off a packed Ibrox.

The following season should have delivered a place in the latter stages of the competition but after taking six points from their opening two matches, Rangers faltered. But the famous wins over Sturm Graz and, in particular, Monaco in Monte Carlo showed Rangers were more than capable of holding their own.

Failure the following season to make the group stages gave rise to a stirring UEFA Cup run under first Advocaat then Alex McLeish.

PSG were beaten on penalties in Paris on a famous night as the club progressed to a last 16 showdown with Feyenoord.

After a 1-1 draw in Glasgow, a breathtaking second leg at De Kuip in Holland saw Rangers take an early lead before eventually going down 3-2 (4-3 on aggregate). Feyenoord would go on to lift the trophy in stunning style, beating Borussia Dortmund 3-2 in a dramatic final.

It proved Rangers were living with the big boys – as did season 2005-06 when the Scottish champions progressed to the last 16 of the fully-revamped Champions League for the first time. A stirring fightback against Porto away from home to earn a point was followed by a battling draw against Inter in Glasgow to put Gers in the knockout stages.

Walter Smith returned for another crack at the top tournament and in 2006-07 the club again almost tasted the rarified air of the last 16 again, narrowly missing out on escaping a group of death that included Barcelona, Lyon and Stuttgart.

The 3-0 win in France with goals from Lee McCulloch, Daniel Cousin and DaMarus Beasley is among the club's greatest nights on foreign soil. Despite taking seven points from their opening three matches, Rangers finished third and dropped down into the 2007-2008 UEFA Cup. But disappointment soon gave way to another famous shot at glory...

MO THE MERRIER Dutch ace Michael Mols enjoys his double against PSV in 1999 in a 4-1 win in Group F with Giovanni van Bronckhorst and Rod Wallace on hand to celebrate

VID YOU BELIEVE IT?
Tony Vidmar, above, celebrates after netting the opener at Ibrox against Parma in August 1999. A 2-0 win made it 2-1 on aggregate as Gers advanced to the Champions League group stages.

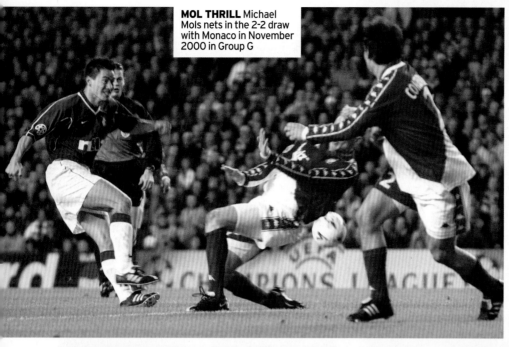

MOL THRILL Michael Mols nets in the 2-2 draw with Monaco in November 2000 in Group G

PEN PALS Dick Advocaat, Arthur Numan, Stefan Klos, Jesper Christiansen and Russell Latapy enjoy the 4-3 shootout win at PSG in the third round of the UEFA Cup in December 2003

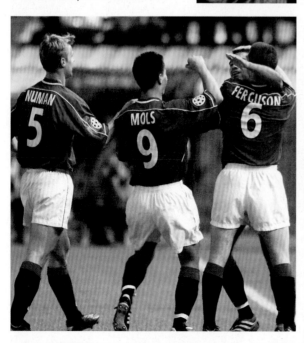

BAZ BOOST Barry Ferguson, right, celebrates his goal in a 3-2 defeat to Feyenoord in the UEFA Cup fourth-round in February 2002 while Gio Van Bronkhurst sinks Monaco in a 1-0 Champions League win in September 2000, above

RON A ROLL Ronald De Boer nets the second goal in the 5-0 win over Sturm Graz in 2000

HIGH FIVE Party time in Group D in September 2000 as the Austrian visitors are crushed

GIO WHIZZ Arthur Numan and Lorenzo Amoruso watch as Gio van Bronckhorst nets in a 3-2 defeat at Galatasaray in September 2000

NER DO WELL Christian Nerlinger celebrates his goal in the 2-1 win over Stuttgart in September 2003 in Group E

ECK OF A DISPLAY Ibrox boss Alex McLeish gives instructions to Chris Burke, Bob Malcolm and Thomas Buffel as Rangers draw 1-1 at home with Inter Milan in Group H of the Champions League in December 2005

DAN FLAIR Gabon striker Daniel Cousin nets in the stunning 3-0 victory in Lyon in the Champions League Group E clash in October 2007

PRSO POWER Dado Prso nets in a stirring 3-2 home win over Porto in September 2005 with Rangers making it out of Group H while, above, Thomas Buffel and Chris Burke celebrate the second goal against Villarreal in the 2-2 Ibrox draw in the last-16 clash in February 2006

LOVEN IT Peter Lovenkrands equalises in the 1-1 draw with Inter Milan in December 2005, right, and then celebrates, above

BARCA BLOCKERS Charlie Adam, Kevin Thomson and Lee McCulloch close down Barcelona's Brazilian magician Ronaldinho in the Champions League Group E match in Glasgow that ended 0-0 in October 2007

DESTINATION MANCHESTER

From the agony of a Champions League exit to the brilliant high
of a trip to the UEFA Cup Final – the glory and the dream of 2008

BREM DE LA CREME Steve Davis celebrates his goal in the 2-0 home win over Werder Bremen in the UEFA Cup fourth round in March 2008

WHEN the final whistle blew on a comprehensive 3-0 defeat at home to Lyon on December 12, 2007 few inside Ibrox Stadium could have imagined the crushing defeat was a good thing.

A place in the Champions League last 16 had been lost despite having seven points from their opening three matches and a spot in the consolation cup seemed like no consolation at all.

How wrong that proved to be as Walter Smith and his battle-hardened squad went on to shake Europe to its core and come within a whisker of lifting the UEFA Cup.

Third place in Champions League group E had secured a UEFA Cup third-round tie against Panathinaikos and Rangers scraped through on the away goals rule.

Ibrox was rocking and the tournament had fully captured Light Blue imaginations by the time German cracks Werder Bremen rolled into town for a last-16 clash which Rangers won 2-0 through goals from Daniel Cousin and midfield battler Steve Davis.

The second leg was negotiated with a 1-0 defeat and suddenly Smith's men were right in the mix.

Sporting Lisbon came calling in the quarters and proved impossible to break down in the firs leg at Ibrox but Rangers upped the ante away from home and a stirring second-half show saw the Scots dump their Portuguese rivals 2-0 thanks to a wonder goal from Steven Whittaker and Jean Claude Darcheville's opener.

The semi-final against Fiorentina was a war of attrition but Rangers stood strong in a second-leg onslaught in Florence to take the tie to penalties where Nacho Novo became the hero as he slotted home the winning spot-kick. Many a tear was shed that night in Italy as Rangers contemplated their first European final since 1972.

Ironically, they found themselves face-to-face with former boss Dick Advocaat as tens of thousands descended on Manchester for a date with Zenit St Petersburg.

With a domestic fixture schedule seemingly set up to hamper the Scottish side's tilt at glory rather than aid it, Rangers went down 2-0 as the Russians struck with two late goals.

The dream had died but the memories lived on and the Ibrox vintage of 2008 had taken their place in the pantheon of Rangers greats.

FLY GUY Daniel Cousin puts Rangers ahead against Werder Bremen in March 2008

SEALED WITH A KISS Steven Naismith seals a semi-final victory after making it 2-0 against Sporting Lisbon in Portugal

NACH OF THE DAY
Nacho Novo nets the crucial strike that sees Gers through on away goals after a 1-1 draw at Panathinaikos in the UEFA Cup third round in February 2008 while Charlie Adam and Werder Bremen's Fritz Clemens tussle in the next round, left, as Gers win 2-0 at Ibrox before progressing 2-1 on aggregate

73

WHIT A NIGHT Steven Whittaker celebrates with a disbelieving Kirk Broadfoot after the 4-2 win on penalties in Florence in May 2008 to clinch a place in the UEFA Cup Final. Nacho Novo, far right with manager Walter Smith, hit the decisive spot kick after the sides were locked at 0-0 on aggregate

FINAL FANTASY Fans celebrate as their side win in Florence to book a place in the Final

YOU'VE AD IT Carlos Cuellar tussles with Adrian Mutu in Florence

WE'LL TAN FIORENTINA Rangers fans enjoy the sun in May 2008 ahead of the UEFA Cup semi-final second-leg clash in Italy

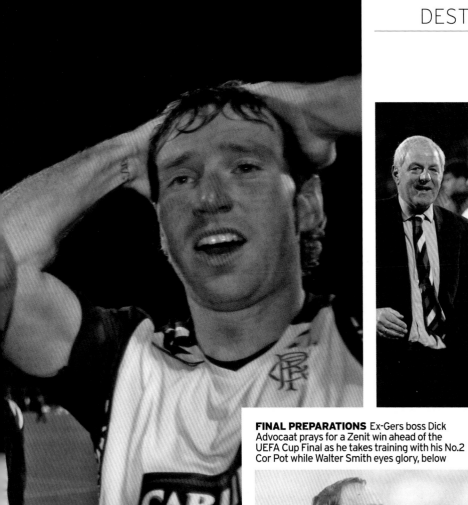

FINAL PREPARATIONS Ex-Gers boss Dick Advocaat prays for a Zenit win ahead of the UEFA Cup Final as he takes training with his No.2 Cor Pot while Walter Smith eyes glory, below